CELSO EMILIO
FERREIRO

Long Night of Stone

Celso Emilio Ferreiro

Long Night of Stone

Translated from Galician by Jack Hill

XUNTA DE GALICIA Small Stations Press

Small Stations Press
Registered address: 20 Dimitar Manov Street, 1408 Sofia, Bulgaria
You can order books and contact the publisher at
www.smallstations.com

Poems and cover photograph © Heirs of Celso Emilio Ferreiro, 2012
English translation © Jack Hill, 2012
Design © Yana Levieva, 2012
© Small Stations Press, 2012
© Xunta de Galicia, 2012

First published in Galician as *Longa noite de pedra* by Editorial Galaxia in 1962

The publishers wish to express their gratitude to the author's family and to Charmian Smy

The poems 'Long Night of Stone,' 'Monologue of an Old Workman,' 'Hunger,' 'Goethe' and 'Incomplete Ballad' appeared in *To Visit Me the Sea* (Hamlet Press, 2000). The poem 'Brothers' appeared in *Anthology of Galician Literature 1196-1981* (Galaxia-Xerais-Xunta de Galicia, 2010)

This English edition first published in 2012, reprinted in 2017
ISBN 978-954-384-011-3 (paperback original)
ISBN 978-954-384-071-7 (reprint edition)
Legal deposit C 591-2012

All rights reserved. The content of this work is protected by the law, which prohibits the reproduction, plagiarism, distribution or public communication, in whole or in part, of a literary, artistic or scientific work, or its transformation, interpretation or artistic performance fixed in any kind of medium or communicated through any means, without the proper authorization

Contents

7	Long Night of Stone
8	A Time to Weep
9	The Kingdom
10	Soldier
14	The Building
16	Spiritual
18	Credo
20	Freely
21	Lament for Carles Riba
23	While We Are Walking
25	Testimony
26	Rabid Dog
27	Pure Air
28	Hope
29	Monologue of an Old Workman
30	Once
31	Words of Advice
32	The Shadow
33	Letter to My Wife
34	Eulogy for the Stonemasons
37	*Cantiga de Amigo* for Joan Miró
39	The Heart of the Wind
41	Formentor
42	Exile
44	The Fable of the Man and the Wolf
47	The Honourable Men
49	The Stone
50	María Soliña
51	It Will Be Here
52	The Silence of God
53	Pessimistic Romance at the End of the Year
55	Baptism of Blood
56	The Tree
57	Don't Look at Me
58	You and Me
59	The Journey Back
60	I Want to Go to Lugo
62	Fragment of a Letter to a Poet Living in Madrid
64	Christmas Eve in Harlem
65	Goethe
66	Municipal Cemetery
67	Prometheus Bound
69	I'm a Halfwit
71	Now Is the Time to Think
72	Winter
73	Roots
74	No
75	Orphan with Horses behind Him
76	Other Names Were Given to Me
77	Fallen by the Sea
79	My Kingdom
80	The Family Grain Store
81	Poetry Is Truth
82	Incomplete Ballad
83	Memory
84	Time Surprised
86	A Poor Man on a City Street
87	Brothers
88	I Can Never Forget
89	Hunger
90	The Oppressed

Long Night of Stone

> *In the middle of the road there was a stone*
> *there was a stone in the middle of the road*
> *there was a stone*
> *in the middle of the road there was a stone.*
>
> Carlos Drummond de Andrade

The roof is stone.
The walls are stone
and the night.
The ground is stone
and the railings.
The doors,
the chains,
the air,
the windows,
the looks,
are stone.
The hearts of men looking outwards
are
also
made of stone.
I too, dying
in this long night
of stone.

A Time to Weep

There is a time to weep without tears a harsh lamentation
for the fettered doves of silver,
for the spirit broken beneath the night
of a strumpeted freedom.
Silent swords are hanging before the eyes
like a cold rain and I must grieve
in the fleeting shadow of this putrefied wind,
which sweeps away loyalty and shackles
the hearts of benevolent men.

Since only my eyes are left to me
to weep for those long rivers,
I must navigate long voyages, discoveries
through times yet to come, full of foam,
and where the day is being born
and there, where the new world is budding.
Since he who weeps is alive, let us go forward,
going, weeping, marching,
a savage voice which has to break out in anger,
in a knife of shouts and reveilles
to mount to the summit of insults.

And since to everything there is a season,
this is the time to weep.

The Kingdom

Then,
when animals could talk,
to say freedom was not sad,
to say truth was like a river,
to say love,
to say friend,
was the same as referring to spring.
No one knew of insults.
When animals could talk,
men would sing in the evenings
of doves of light and goldfinches of dream.
To say yours and mine was not comprehensible,
to say sword was prohibited,
to say prison was only a word
without meaning, a breath which missed
the heart of the people.

When,
when was it lost,
that great Kingdom?

Soldier

> *George, you old debutante,*
> *How did you get in the Army?*
>
> W. H. Auden, *For the Time Being*

I

His blue eyes were full of questions
about weather and harvests. His mind was
with the reapers singing at dusk, at the start
of evening, when the night became like a lover.
He didn't understand high-flown terms,
nor words full of solemn pride,
nor men of stupid self-sufficiency
who considered themselves important
because their ancestors had come to be gentry
by way of self-prostitution, genuflection and corruption.
He listened to the talk of duty to the sovereign state,
of sacred institutions, of order, of glory,
and he remembered occasionally the oak tree
by the door of his cottage, high in the mountains,
by the river which murmured the continuous elegy
of ripples on stone; he remembered as well
the ragged suit of the blond-haired teacher
who went to war one day and never came back;
and he also remembered the baggage of emigrants
and the flight of swallows across the sun.
His heart was full of little local words
like tiny homelands or fluttering heartbeats.
Illiterate and simple, he watched the wisdom
of the woods and interpreted the deep-voiced
wind growling in the night. He spoke

his old-fashioned words slowly and then fell quiet to listen
to the silence
of the world, immense and laid out like a plain.
He opened his farm labourer's hands,
which now grasped a gun,
and stared at them stubbornly, slowly.

II

Suddenly on the far limits of the horizon
glowed the brilliance of a city in flames
like a distant yellow threat.
The noise of bombardment fell from above
like the deafening bellow of a raging river,
a hoarse din smothering the landscape.
A dog howled somewhere on the outskirts
and the flashes of lightning started.
Smoke
like a gigantic palm tree
opened its burning arms
and spattered a dark announcement of death
across the celestial dome.
Whistles and flashes of lightning.
Evening birds
dropped dead as autumn leaves.
A factory siren started to wail
and split into two pieces the warm day,
the humid intimate day, tasting of kisses.
Flashes of lightning.
     (A light bulb went on.)
Deformed hands, knuckles emphasized,
stretched in the trembling air
and an altarpiece of bloodless faces,
staring at the sky, accused the gods.

Burnt flesh, legs, feet, horseshoes...
An ambushed bull, like a Minotaur lost
in a labyrinth of arms, faces, legs, swollen breasts,
bellowed incessantly.
      (A light bulb went off.)
A broken chisel
proclaimed its protest.
A horse, lost, unbridled, galloped frantically
on hoofs of stone and nitroglycerine.
Flashes of lightning.
It stank like a pigsty mixed with shit and sulphur.
      (A light bulb went on, then off.)
You could see, and not see, a landscape
of arms, faces, legs, fingers,
roof-tiles, breasts, doors, wires...
Flashes of lightning and the last gunfire.
Then nothing. Silence. The heavy silence
of a snowy night or untilled earth.
George, you old debutante,
who are with those who suffer history
and against those who write it,
how did you get in the Army?

III

They got to the outskirts of the city,
covered with ash and fatigue.
The lieutenant shouted, 'Halt, who goes there?';
amaryllis grew in an immense solitude.
The silence of the starry night
was an infinite white highway.
Cartridge belts went ting-a-ling,
ting-a-ling, in time to the march.
A raw recruit, flat as a patient in hospital,
stared at the unpitying sky,
a rifle in one hand,
a bag in the other.
The son of his mother was dead,
gloriously dead in a bog.
He had wind in his eyes. He was asking
with the blue eyes of a tame animal.
George, you old, you eternal debutante,
tell me what you're thinking.

The Building

The telegram city got dirty
one Monday morning at twelve:
an urgent assembly,
defence, development,
investment, finance, dividends.
The monster opened its mouth:
it produced the argument
for offering new victims to the gods.
It produced the words which destroy
the light-bringers, the heralds:
death penalty,
                life imprisonment,
                              charge-sheet.
Standing as one, the convocation,
knives in their eyes,
proclaimed the law of tunnel vision
with an affirmative yes in D major.
(A favourable
rise in share prices came next.)
Contracts were signed with a flourish,
they started to erect
the building, the prison of dreams,
the great house of fear.
On every stone blood, drop by drop,
on every column sadness and tears,
wrath on the capitals,
stupidity on the arches.
And above, on the outside,
standing on zest and hope,
a deaf caryatid presiding.

People forgot their names,
assumed the aliases of war.
All one heard was talk of light
and the interpreters of the great book
said fine, all that
had been foreseen, was good
in the eyes of the gods
and had the favourable approval of the Eumenides.

Spiritual

Perhaps tomorrow,
when my glance
doesn't come out in the light
like a little water poppy,
I shall feel homesick.

But today I sing in freedom
and, as I sing,
I am not alone,
for the heart goes with me
and with it I speak.

I shall drink the landscape
in a dawning of lilies.
The church bells of the sea
in the fugitive winds.

Each moment a bird,
each pulse a heartbeat.
A sword of rain
cutting the flower of the wind.

No black looks,
no lying kisses,
no hostile voices,
no worthless men.

I shall live like a light
lit in the darkness.
I shall have summits of stars,
I shall sing for men.

I am with myself.
The heart gives its orders
and I obey.

Credo

I believe that this world is very fertile
and that there are some hydroelectric rivers,
but that the bellies of grieving mothers
could be heaps of wheat,
that I can never believe.

I believe that the moon is that thing
on the roof of the night,
but that the aircraft which goes drone, drone,
bellyaching up there, could be an insect,
that I can never believe.

I believe that men sin seven times
seven times seven every day,
I believe in geometry,
I believe in the diminutive atom,
but that there can be human beings
capable of reading the papers in tranquillity
without a gut-feeling of revulsion,
that I can never believe.

Changing the subject, I say, for example:
Elizabeth, a cyclone made in USA,
sowed the Caribbean with corpses.
Cluster bombs, boom and tyrannies,
a black lynched in Little Rock, Arkansas,
the rights of man in cold war.

Changing the subject, for the sake of example:
what a huge disgrace it is to be a poet
with the office of weeping for free,
the office of spitting into the enormous sea,
of whacking up placards in the desert.
(Conformist poets in this world
– testicular emporium of skeletons –
while mankind struggles, weeps and suffers,
carry on singing of the violet, the daisy,
pulling off the leaves of the recalcitrant rose
of your minimal problems,
say yes to everything and thrive.)

Changing the subject to say etcetera,
etcetera, you get it, under my breath
with ellipses
to cover the prohibited words
struggling to emerge from me,
which do come out of me
with forceps of hatred and foul temper:
there is something rotten in the state of Denmark
and it stinks to high heaven.

Finally I shall intone a great *Te deum
laudamus* of optimism to say thank you
to the mighty sky,
which framed me just as you see me,
an abandoned stone, a trembling thing,
a conduit of time and sleep. I say a man.

Freely

We wanted freely
to eat our daily bread. Freely
to bite it, chew it, fearlessly digest it,
freely talking, singing on the banks
of rivers freely running down to the sea.
Freely, freely
we wanted only
to be freely men, to be stars,
to be sparks from the great fireplace of the world,
to be ants, birds, boys,
in the Noah's ark on which we row.
We wanted freely to smile,
to speak of it to God in the passing wind
– in the long wind of the woods and plains –
without fear, without blackness, without chains,
without sin, freely, freely,
like the air of the morning and spray.
Like the wind.
But this our difficult love was broken
– the glass of a fragile dream –
on a reef of screams
and now we are no more than shadows.

Lament for Carles Riba

Elder brother. Standard-bearer
of us who toil in the mystery
of the living word
and wrestle with no truce
against the angel and the night.

Gentle grape-harvester
of that Attic root-stock
by the side of the sea of hope
and the warm evenings of gulls
in sweet Catalonia, the mountain land.

I wish for you a joyful crown
woven of moon and wave,
woven of wind and spray,
music of the clean water
which inspires the cadence of the mills
in the fields of this my old land,
peaceful and peaceless,
so lamented in impotent tears.

May the myrtle and laurel bind up your dreams,
your distant flowing rivers,
rain-betrayed heart.

Now you already have your hands
full of the seeds of the impossible miracle,
tell me if at the end it was certain
what the stones spoke of
like mad augurs of nowhere when,

flying over the empty fields,
you achieved the islands
which the sea had left you as legacy.

And tell me more; send me more news:
if it is certain that we are alive,
if it is certain that memory
matures us for death
or for a meaningful life
and, more meaningful yet,
a heart seized by surprise,
that the shade was worthwhile
both in fire and play
and in melancholy.

While We Are Walking

Time smells the railway station
on the outskirts of daybreak,
when the trains groan and gallop
through tunnels of night
and shine mysterious lights
into the deep woods
and the confused profile of far-off cities.
While we are walking.

Time plays the lonely shepherd's
melancholy flute; the Jew's harp of the wind
in the yellow acacias at the fall of dusk.
A monotone sound
which comes down in fits and starts from the hills,
gets to the valley and turns into a bird.
While we are walking.

Time is the colour of meadows, but sometimes
puts on crimson glasses and shines
– colourless, dark, moonlit –
like a Sahara of restless sand;
a water of sand, a rain of sand,
over interminable oceans of sand.
While we are walking.

Time carries pennants of shouts hung
on barbed wire; brings crannies of light;
brings the rags of hope hoisted
on masts of dreams; brings the last words

of the unknown soldiers
who died in battles for futile fatherlands.
While we are walking.

Time is a thing which is there, which destroys
like a long snake tracking down
the heart of men, those tapeworms
who are passing and were passing,
scrabbling to break through a strong wall of longing
with the stone of dark gods marking out their shadow.
While we are walking.

While we are walking, time has a name,
an alias of snow which no one can pronounce,
an alias which weeps on the windows of winter,
on the secret gardens of underwater holly.
While we are walking, I ask for the dead,
I ask for the colours of the flowers they loved,
I ask for the tender mornings they enjoyed,
I ask for the waves of the sea. I ask.
While we are walking.

Testimony

I present the testimony of wounds
– destroyed youth,
cut flower of ambition –
and dedicate myself to the dark cries of the roadways.
Look how we are mutilated,
rotten stumps raised
in an interminable night.
See the long soft shadows
run by, death-faced,
the silent bishopric of that day
– Day of the Unknown Grief –
yet to be written on the stars.
I present the testimony of insults
and dedicate myself to the fear of the first men
who lit beacons on the hill-tops
and believed in the liberty of dreams.

Rabid Dog

Like a mad dog on the road,
terror is on the loose through the world.

It looks like a black wind closing
its crow's wings
over the heads of fearful men.

A winter frost in the open
paralyses the clock, stabs the throat,
puts veils of privation on words.

A huge telescope watches us,
like a Cyclops eye
following our footsteps,
stares without rest at our journey,
from every window,
from every watch-tower,
from every voice which speaks to us.

Night is an impassive microphone
listening to our heartbeat
like a dark unseen spy seeing
into our innermost thoughts.
Everything turns into something unavowable;
behind every corner a suspicion,
a doubt behind every shadow
and fear, fear, fear,
a bottomless well of fear,
a mirror of cold water
in which terror stares at itself for eternity.

Pure Air

The pure air of morning proclaims
its right to come into every house.

Patria, open your doors to it!
Soul, give your breasts to it!
Quit the acid darkness which plagues you,
forget those shrouds,
dry your tears,
speak,
sing,
put away despair,
don't let them insult you; you insult them.

Not now. Think of the days
yet to come, drop the memories
which tie you down.
Let the bright morning
into your house.

Hope

Let us raise hope
over this dark land
like raising a beacon
on a moonless night.

Let us march arm in arm
through the harsh secrets
of a dreamed-of country
to which we shall not return.

They won't know the way
which we shall take.
The long rivers of mists,
the long seas of time.

We, the sleepless crewmen,
we believe in liberty.
Bravo, bravo, we say
to those who live in exile
and dream of a dawning
of banners in the breeze.

Addicts of yearning
bearing light along the pathways,
a health to you all,
companions!

Monologue of an Old Workman

Now I sit in the sun. Till now
I worked fifty years without stopping.
Day in, day out, I ate my bread,
sweating in endless work on the farm.
I wasted my time on Saturday's money
and spring went by and winter came.
I gave the boss the flower of my strength
and my youth. I have nothing.
The boss is rich at my expense
and I, at his, am old.
If you think about it properly, he owes me everything.
I don't even owe him
the sun I'm sitting in now.

While I'm sitting in it, I hope.

Once

Once there lived a man
who never said 'mine'!
He knocked on the door of the world,
he called in my heart.
He spoke in words
which seemed to be doves.
Things at his side
turned white.
There was born in his eyes
a dawn like a river of light,
like a distant ocean of sea birds.
That man had
a balsam of love
for this
my nameless grief.

Words of Advice

After Proverbs 23:1-9

If you should dine with the mighty,
consider diligently what is before you.
Hobble your appetite, cut back the sweetmeats,
shut the doors of hunger should you have it,
for the bread of the rich is a bread of deception,
sweet on the surface, bitter within.
Throttle ambition,
do not trouble to approach to those riches.
Do you not know that gold is worth nothing,
brought by the wind and as soon blown away?
Do not break bread with a man who's ignoble,
nor envy him the size of his fortune.
He will say, 'Eat and drink, my bosom companion,
enjoy my possessions as much as you want to,'
but his thoughts do not go with the words he is saying,
the words of his mouth may be outwardly open,
but his heart, hardened and wicked,
always keeps bolted
the windows of love and justice.

Do not forget.

The Shadow

Shadow of Prometheus bound,
the boy I was is already dead.

I look for a clean land. Now I look
for an unbloodied land not to be found.

Distant spring. I hear voices
in the starry night. Long rivers.
Where are you now, my heart of yesterday,
that light heart never to be seen again?

I ask and you do not answer, black death.
Where did it go, that joyful life?

I only have you, my memory
wrapped in solitudes and nostalgia:
patterings of raindrops weeping
over a window of dreams.

I plod across the mud of the world.
I endlessly mourn for that boy.

Letter to My Wife

My darling, always remember there are words
it is a sin to utter at this time.
Words you must never pronounce,
nor even think, meditate,
stammer, praise, write…
much less shout.
My wife, take note and don't forget:
don't say liberty, a sad word
with danger of death and a skull.
If you really love me, never say
that stupid word
which has teeth and bites like a wolf.
Don't even say
the words derived from it,
however distant and vague
may be their etymological parentage,
such as library, libertine,
libidinous, liberated woman, free exchange.

Instead say bondage, hurrah, hurrah,
yes sir, no sir, three bags full sir, God bless you!

Now you see how happy we're going to be!

Eulogy for the Stonemasons

*But now I am thinking
of the workman
who fixed the roof.*

Cassiano Ricardo, *Martim Cererê*

I

First came the sea and then the stone
forming its crust under
the original wind and light.
    The word of God
opened the closed night
on that morning of beginning,
diastole and systole,
in coagulations of the heartbeats of rock.
Tectonic impulses
lifted the geological barrier,
the stone architecture of mother earth,
the foundation structure of the mountains,
cradle of the sun, witness of epochs,
the stream of the seven unseen rivers.
    Everything happened.
Impregnating rains and tempests,
steppes covered with mosses and lichens,
the initial claps of thunder.
And the mammoths.

But the stone remained the backbone of the world,
the forceful prow of the ship,
the mystery of the principles
in which sleep the forms
as a dark melody sleeps
in the unvoiced music of silence.

II

From the grooved flint of the cave
to the dolmen of Cornwall,
to Easter Island,
to marbled Greece,
to the Sphinx,
to the august portico of Mateo,
passing by the walls
which mark out the ancient hill-forts,
which build the thatched kraals and monasteries.
Passing by the arches and columns,
capitals and domes,
mouldings and architraves,
archivolts and gargoyles,
can be seen
the enspiréd hond of the craftesmon
at his intens labor, peece-mele
the manere, wel, wel graven,
of the skilful artesan.

While there are men on earth,
while there are nichtes in time,
the stanes shall speak.
                    The ciseles, the maletes,
sing, create, build, lead the stone,
they raise the cities and kirkes,
the groundewerk, the wals, the keystanes.
The world is a stone,
the roads are pavéd with cobles
and fire, that thing from heaven,
burns above the slated housen of the thorpe.
Stanes with Lord Jesus nailéd on the cross
and his moder birefte weping at his fote.

Stanes overal,
stanes beneth,
under the streme like ronde miroirs,
further on than al grete rivers,
further on yet to the oceanes flod.
Powerful thews of the crafts of the maçons
which bear up the comely and auncién̄t cites
like ghostly ships of the night
when the mon beginneth to shed al hir rays.
You are the flower of honoured men,
the skin of those who work
for their daily bread
and have their hands calloused
by their noble labour.
Caste of poets,
little gods, constructors
of the refuges which keep us
from the rain and snow,
of the shepherd huts where we are born,
we copulate, we die.
Be in the hands of the Master Almighty,
may he give you a paradise of stone,
blue and pink and white,
sweet as an autumn garden,
with a long river singing beside it.

Cantiga de Amigo for Joan Miró

Cantiga de amigo *was a medieval troubadour verse-form in which a woman speaks of her love*

I hail Joan Miró,
who made me see the long shadows
of sweet and melancholy post-horns
which had been before me without my seeing,
flowering with autumns as ever,
singing their song from the beginning.

I hail Joan Miró,
who taught me to see the untranscended
beneath the stones and folk-songs,
in the painful dreams of adolescence,
down there, where words come together
in clusters of inconcrete questions.

I hail Joan Miró,
who knows how to reconcile opposing light
and calculate the sad eternal forces
which drive the tides and solstices,
which bring the oaks to flourish and move
the grief of children lost in cities.

I hail Joan Miró,
the algebraic and homesick eremite,
the weaver of impossible contours,
who keeps time in amphoras of wind,
tight-lipped, curved, golden, metaphysical,
with a young camellia in his eyes.

From this fog-wrapped shore
of hovering light like a caress,
where the sea turns to river and kisses
the dolmen of old pagandoms, I send you,
Joan Miró, an embrace. I long for
your south, the simple clarity
of spray at midday, the distant blue
of your native land, exact and strong.

The Heart of the Wind

Ángel Ferrant, the heart of the wind
is a peaceful tele-twit of a sputnik,
a blue and never-painted apple,
a fugitive fish.
It is tired.
From that soft paradise tree,
from primeval clay,
from the first breathing mud
to the grey roofs of Hiroshima
– my unconsoled love –
the heart of the wind is no comfort.
It is tired.
Under the ants there are wires,
there are docile smiling skulls
under a rain of lead
– ta-ta-ta, ta-ta-ta – in the red dawn.
Under the snowflakes,
under the timorous footsteps,
there are skewers piercing, pierce, pierce,
penetrating the will of free men.
The heart of the wind, hung out
from the window of morning
or endless roof of the closed night,
is a warm bird,
is a dove
saying farewell to the sky from the roadways.
It is tired.
Ángel Ferrant, you know the bellowing
quickly turned into swords
or insomniac screwdrivers

or sonorous potatoes
or mystical parrots
with a soul of cypress and guitar.
If you know, tell me, tell me
that the soft heart of the wind
is tired.

Formentor

Under the sea sounds a tambourine
and there is an underwater river of light.
Above the sea sounds a flute
and there is a street of white camellias.
They come to the south,
they come to the clear skies.

A blue air of gentle butterflies
flutters, soft and persistent, from boat to boat.
I see an income of sea spray in my eyes
and have young blood in my arms.
Here was an Eden of soft clay,
here were born all the birds.
And every highway that carried
myrtles and mirrors came through here.
I am in the south,
I am in the clear skies.
This is an island of mysterious caves,
Formentor is its beacon.
Anointed with old olives,
its night has distant lights,
voices, crystals, silent woods,
glow-worms and stud-farms.

I come from the south,
I come from the clear skies.
Aquamarines were born in my hands,
I bear orange blossom on my lips.

Exile

I turned on the bath tap
and the water came
sneezing out,
a-ti-shoo.
(City water doesn't sing.)
'Old girl friend,
comrade
of a faraway childhood
in the mountains,
what are you doing
in this house?'
'I am in jail,
they have me in exile.
Bars of black iron
press on my soul.
Under the city,
down by the sewers,
my night goes by
with never a dawn.
Butterflies in autumn,
under a drizzle,
whatever became of
the leaves turning golden
I used to carry on me?
Mirror of starlight
and passing clouds
in brooks that sang
mad with white spindrift?
What became of that sky,
of the wind and skylarks,

of those silent sunsets,
of meadows and ploughlands?'
'Just like me,
sister water,
I too have yearning
for my own country,
to which I shall go back
one day in a coffin.
You can't turn time back,
it passes, not to return.
The sea is still waiting.
The sea.
The night without dawn.'

The Fable of the Man and the Wolf

I

A man came running out of the burning city
and took the path to the outlying hills,
where stood the country houses of the rich.
He had two grenades hanging on his belt
and carried a smoking machine-gun.

He ran like a madman until he threw himself,
breathless, down at the foot of a willow tree,
having stared into the distance,
into the frontier of night,
at the blazing fire
like a distant bleeding daybreak.

Gradually he fell asleep under the high stars
while by his side the toad
sounded its magic flute and a chorus of crickets
orchestrated their anthem.

II

Along the path lost in the blackness
of night tentatively stepped a wolf
with the gift of human speech, as used to happen
in the millennial times of the beginning of the world.
It spoke, 'Brother man.'
'I'm not your brother and I don't want to be.'
'You are my brother, though the pain

of knowing it eats your guts out. You are my brother
and only thus do I understand
the daybreak of light in the distant city.'
'It's war. You can't understand. War
is the dynamic of our ideals. War
for honour, for liberty, for civilization.'
'Of course I understand. You kill each other for words.'
'Yes, words, which are the seed of a better world.'
'Be quiet. You say you're fighting for honour
and you get yourselves filthy with dishonour. You say
you're fighting for liberty and you put your enemies in chains.
You say you're defending civilization and you destroy it.
Man, you who invented logic, what logic is that?'
'Force is the mailed fist of logic. Man needs
both force and logic.'
'Oh yes, I know. You need logic
to justify force and force to justify
your logic.'
'What right do you have to speak to me
like that, wolf? You kill as the primary instinct
of your life. And you kill, motivated
by demented homicide.'
'We are born good, but the world makes us bad.'
'Discredited old wives' tales. The world
is bad because it is made by you.'
'I am a superior being.'
'The first among animals of prey.'
'You don't know me. If you knew my tormented heart,
you'd think different.'
'There was a man who said the more
he got to know you, the better he liked his dog.'

III

The night was as tuneful as the sea.
The flautist toad timed its song
to the counterpoint of the crickets.
A wakening wind measured the mime
of its flight to the stirring of the branches.
Suddenly morning opened its door
to the grace of the sun and began
to turn the hill-tops to gold,
to gild the blue distance.
A twitter of birds burst
from the wood and the roads filled
with the noise of the crowds fleeing
a city turned into flame and iron.
The man with the bombs and machine-gun
got up, stretched
and continued running.

The Honourable Men

I am an honourable man.
(I never went hungry.)
You are an honourable man.
(You never went hungry.)
Yes, honour conjugated
in satisfactory verbs,
nourished, polished, full.
Ah, pot-bellied honour,
the loyal horse,
the labouring ant,
the virtue of the civil servant,
the lineage of the well-born
grandsons of noble servants.

But when I bear injustices
nailed to my feet like knives;
when in the night
my eyes perforate the roofs;
when the wind brings a song
to my isolated sleep;
when bread turns into a star
and fear hammers nails
endlessly into my heartbeat every day;
then I am not so honourable.

When time is called economy
and is tangled up in work for money;
when on every notice a mermaid
sells illusions for banknotes
and powerful machines shatter

arms and legs to dust;
when an imprecise dawn arrives
and goes from flower to flower
and turns itself into weeping,
converts itself into ashless fire;
then you are not so honourable.

The Stone

She-wolf, you ask for my children
to bind them
to the long twilight of your interminable
death.
You ask for my children
for the crime
of your unconquerable sword.
You give me, in exchange, silence,
you give me jail
and fear.
You darken life,
you poison time,
shameless slut giving yourself
to the dirty passions of the powerful.
You ask for my sons,
arms,
legs,
eyes.
You neuter me,
you batter me,
you gut me.
You make me a slave,
a thing crying ash.

But my heart
will never be yours,
you bloody whore
sold
for the bosses'
gold.

María Soliña

Along the roads of Cangas
the wind's voice was wailing:
ah, left lonely little
María Soliña.

Upon the sands of Cangas
the walls of night were rising:
ah, left lonely little
María Soliña.

The sea-waves of Cangas
bitter echoes were drinking:
ah, left lonely little
María Soliña.

The seagulls over Cangas
dreams of fear were weaving:
ah, left lonely little
María Soliña.

Beneath the roofs of Cangas
walks a terror of cold water:
ah, left lonely little
María Soliña.

It Will Be Here

In memory of Aquilino Iglesia Alvariño

I want to die here (when comes
the hour of the voyage that awaits me).
Here, in this silence
of nesting doves,
in this wind which sleeps in the pine trees
a deep sleep of longings.
I want to die here, my eyes set
on the smoking chimneys, on the cinders
of time face to face
with me, my soul open
to the hill-tops of hours, in a night
sounding with harps.
The wandering clouds come and go,
swallows pass by.
The tambourine of rain
embroiders a sweet song
of autumn timed to
the bagpipe chanter of the river.
I want to die here. Be sown
into my own surroundings.
To finish here my bitter weariness,
to fold here for ever my wings.

The Silence of God

In the slow daybreaks
full of doubtful lights,
the silence of God is like a boat
sweetly navigating my eyes.

They hurt me, all those things
beneath the implacable rain
which falls on the dark crust of this world.

A winter pain,
a pain of the cold fields far away,
loads knives of wind
onto the last flight of birds.

The silence of God blends with the mist
and weighs on my eyelids. I ask.
An immense wall
limits the voices of those weeping mud.

Pessimistic Romance at the End of the Year

Time passes unceasingly,
an infinite river of silence,
an infinite river, night and day,
an infinite river, black and white.
In its mills of the day
it mills the flower of my contentment.
In its mills of the night
my heart is being milled.
A long and starlit river
with neither end nor beginning.
One mill for yearning,
one for grief and fear,
one for all sad memories
of hours already dead.
Hours leaving ship-wakes
of love in the heart.
The days had a name
and the names had a meaning
Time to speak of snow,
time to say our prayers,
time to close our eyes,
time to water the fields.
Father was talking war,
mother was making a comment,
son was watching the world,
his astonished eyes open.
What became of those snows,
warm voice of my elders?
What became of the flowers of yesteryear,
blue eyes of childhood?

Run on, infinite river,
dark mill-race of silence.
Run on by, dark water,
taking everything with you.
Now I hardly care
whether I am distant or close,
for though I live in this world,
I keep my heart in exile.
The banners taken down,
now nothing has meaning.
Conquered, I continue walking,
not knowing where I'm going.
Every day the same.
Awaiting nothing, unbelieving,
with no reason to hurry,
I am neither sad nor happy
and if I start to sing,
I must sing as I want to,
infinite river, night and day
infinite river, black and white:
Little star, the star of Venus,
giving so much light and truth,
the day and the night have gone,
so have my boyhood and youth.

Baptism of Blood

When I was an automaton, years back,
my feet and my greetings were electric.
The landscape was weeping in long plains
with clusters of dead men unburied.
(One, two, eyes left.)
The patria throbbed in my wrists.
(One, two, quick march.)
The air was wrapped in a dark event
of childhood in the oak trees.
Endlessly walking through the smoke
with forests of rifles over my eyes.
And under the night a hidden fear,
an adolescent fear which wounded,
which raged in the groin, dark, dumb,
like a cobra dragged out by the blood.
The chief was on horseback. There were walls
deep in shadow.
Everything was far away. The world itself
was far away. (Hit the deck.)
Seed which bore the fruit
of solitude at the end of a road.
The abandoned kid had already grown up.
(Dismiss, one, two.)
It was the flesh of love between two furrows.

The Tree

Death is like a tree
sown with one, born with us
when we are born, with the first
of our tears in our eyes.
A tree born in us on the left hand
of the longest road of night.
When I die, I'll see it, I'm sure,
one single leafless tree
climbing up before me to the sky
like hands in prayer
at the bottom of a plain.
A single tree, a tree
naked before the night,
growing, will go on growing, growing,
till my eyes are crammed with ants.

Don't Look at Me

Now I've seen everything.
What I saw one day
weighs on my eyelids like a stone.
The burden of seeing, by God it hurts.
I saw wolves growing,
I saw fences arising,
I saw ashes coming down
in the bloody mill-streams.
I went as far as volcanoes;
I had fire in my hands.
I saw, going by, silent files
of boys made men too quickly.
Splosh, splosh, their boots
sploshed over the mud.
I saw men condemned to death
with yellow cloths wrapping
their faces like skulls.
I saw roads crammed with dead
staring at the sky, asking.
I saw God in chains. I saw liberty yoked.
I saw false paradises
of jeers and injustice.
I saw slaves singing.
My eyes wound. Don't look at them.

You and Me

(Don't let's talk of the idiots
who learn everything from books.
Don't let's talk of the cretins
with Sunday faces,
nor of the knowledgeable halfwits,
nor of the clever bully-boys,
nor of the eternal bad taste
of the poor nouveaux riches.)

Let us talk of you and me
while we're still alive.

You and me in the winds
and solstices.

You and me in the woods
and rivers.

You and me, history
of clean bodies.

You and me, longing
of intimate trees.

You and me with no time for
the time we are going.

You and me singing,
weeping, laughing.

The Journey Back

I got to the valley. I came down from the mountains
and I swear I have seen nothing new:
only your pure breasts, springtime.

I saw the same traitors,
the same accusers,
the same rubbish collectors,
the same usurers,
hustlers, shit-inks, pederasts.
As old as the world. Nothing new.
Only your pure breasts, springtime.

I would like to say why I feel fed up
in this valley of conformist butchers.
I saw hundreds of men die.
I saw women give birth,
I saw the arrival of justice after a time.
I saw flooded rivers of blood,
I saw enormous walls of ignorance.
Walls of greed,
walls of avarice,
walls of hypocrisy.
Walls
as old as the world.
Nothing new.
Only your pure breasts, springtime.

I Want to Go to Lugo

Remarked José Terra, my brother-in-exile,
the poet and helmsman of the mist:

> *The day after the day after tomorrow*
> *I shall go with my friend to Glasgow...*

In Glasgow, say I, the wind is probably green
and sleeps in a cradle of gulls.
In Glasgow the men are odd, very odd,
and probably live beyond the law of gravity.

But I don't want to go to Glasgow,
neither tomorrow or ever, my friend, José Terra,
as there's too much to see in my own country.
I want to go to Lugo
to lose myself in the streets of water,
in the village roads at twilight,
in the squares full of red-cheeked children
singing with the church bells,
with the last lights from the windows.

To walk through the neighbouring fields
outside the high walls of dreams
which enclose the old heart of the city.

A mistletoe-coloured sky
over the corrugated iron roofs
covered by bracken in the morning
with father river rumbling and bubbling
by the bank, looking for ships.

I want to go to Lugo
to walk past the sleepless doors
one by one
under the weathercocks waiting for the moon,
knowing of the sacred woods of the olden days
and the humble secrets of the violets.
To speak of our things:

of the lands of nowhere,
of non-existent islands,
of the tree of foam,
of hobgoblins, of the phoenix,
of weeping fishes.

And then slowly,
in the contemporary voice,
to speak of the grief of the men watching us,
of the heartbeats of lead in our ears,
of the hands tied to the wheels of cars
bidding farewell to the smoke
rising sadly from the roofs.

Fragment of a Letter to a Poet Living in Madrid

… now you see, my friend,
what a sad life we have.

But if to that you add the newspapers
with a weekly football supplement,
the obituaries (half a page)
of the fat-bellied bourgeois who died
in all dignity and the posthumous honour
of the most illustrious gentleman who now rests in peace,
his most excellent wife inconsolable,
and other various special advantages,
you will well understand: one is not at peace.
But you arrived at your ease,
your heart very attentive, your ideas
the same. All ready
to observe things and turn them into poetry
(so as not to cry) and contradict them,
call them by their prohibited names
and build them over the putrefying air.

You arrived, Gabriel, humane,
simply speaking to the stars,
and everything has become more beautiful,
more clear and more profound.
Time now, far off,
announces morning
and orders hope.

I hope. Every day we must hope
to start again.
We have to begin:
from century to century it is known
one has always to begin again.

The unsleeping rose of the heart commands us
and we obey. This is the lesson.

We shall sing. We have to wait singing,
conquering the repugnance of living in a cellar,
dominating the ancient weariness,
with our hearts in our hands, I say, in their place.

Christmas Eve in Harlem

At the foot of a photograph in Life

At the gate of the roads
they are hoisting pennants of dreams.
At the gate of daybreak are men
with a stone of snow before their eyes.
> In the backstreets of the world there, in Harlem,
> flow rivers of dawns and flags.
> In the backstreets of dreams,
> rivers of crowds and stars.

They are waiting for a new beginning to wake the night
of distant grandfathers made of darkness.
A new beginning of swallows
for the liberty of man, which never comes.
> The side-drum of the woods patters
> in the blood in counterpoint with heartbeats.

The side-drum of the plains
throbs now in forests of cement.
All together on earth. Beneath the sky
rise the sweet morning and gentle night.
All together in the world,
all together on the same Christmas Eve.

The liberty of God breaks chains
and quietens the blues of the slaves.
The liberty of all,
for all men, black and white.

Goethe

That bourgeois gentleman smothered in decorations,
His very fat Lordship or Excellency,
who snores with pleasure all night,
has a happy wife with oblong tits,
two sons, weaklings, sports fans,
a bit randy, and noisy piss-up artists
getting their stupidity from mum
and their flab from dad;
that señor showing his teeth
like a dog with a bone
starts to growl and bites:
'I prefer injustice to disorder.'

Municipal Cemetery

The pride of the powerful stretches to the cemetery,
turns into Corinthian marble
and proprietorial bronze.
>We should publicly wave this placard:
>there are first-class dead, second-class dead
>and the dead who don't have anywhere to drop dead.

A rich man's skeleton
is worth treble that
of simple men who pick up on Saturday
a derisory wage of dreams and hopes.
The powerful dead
have a ticket to the royal box in the graveyard
and recline in a grotto of separatist marble,
thinking that the trumps of the Last Judgement
will exclusively sound for them
a beautiful and prosperous reveille.
>One day we shall sweep away this offensive earth
>and build a single egalitarian tomb.
>We shall throw in the sea the poisonous marble,
>melt the arrogant bronze in the fire.
>We shall send the mighty bones of their ancestors
>to their descendants for them to speculate
>>on the markets
>with nitrates, iron, carbon and copper,
>so they can live, as ever, off investments.

Prometheus Bound

He was lost in the city of cells
one birdless winter morning.
In the city of chains,
of bundles of dead.

>   Alas this house!
>   All were silent.

Behind every window a dark face
with sad eyes was watching the road.
Over the naked souls of the vanquished
soundlessly pattered the rain.

>   Alas this house!
>   All were silent.

A long wall echoed voices
hoarse with horror and fear.
In the city of chains,
a morning of hanged men.

>   Alas this house!
>   All were silent.

Traveller: Sir, where is the road?
Worthy citizen: I know nothing.
Traveller: Please, guard, where is the road
leading to free air,
the freedom of the wind,
open fields,
the beautiful sea?

Guard: I don't know the road, traveller.
Traveller: How come? A guard
must know the roads.
Guard: And if I did know the roads,
do you think I'd be stuck here as a guard?
Worthy citizen: I know nothing, I want
to know nothing.

    Alas this house!
    All were silent.

I'm a Halfwit

I'm a halfwit
walker
with an opinion,
telling the bare truth
in the street.
I never was a user
of luxury cars
or even utility ones.
I walk on foot,
which is why
I see the world as it is.
I know bourgeois greed
and proletarian fury.
Bread stays in the bin,
hunger circles daily.
I don't rush,
nothing changes my timetable
or cuts off my commentary.
I'm not afraid
of what time may bring
because I know that,
sooner or later,
what will be will be.
Right time, wrong time?
So what?
Oh to be alive
when it happens!
What a joy
to see what's coming come.

For that great event
already, far over there,
is lit a light
which will catch in the world
and burn off
all the stinking rot.
I walk on foot,
which is why
I can see the world as it is.

Now Is the Time to Think

When I think that I'm protected
against wind and rain,
against bullets and bombs,
by a roof of optimistic words;
when I think that mine is the light of dawn,
mine is the smoke at night,
mine are the high roads and butterflies;
when I think I have four children
with the right to grow up or more precisely
with the right to be meat for this world's sharks;
when I think I appear
on the pages of the civil and parochial records,
on the pages of the military and trade union records,
on the pages of the police and civil guard records,
on the pages of the justiciary and public authority records,
and that I go through the world legally
with documents accrediting that I am who I am
and not some other bastard with an illegitimate identity;
when I think that I think
and in that much I exist,
although sometimes more dead than alive,
for no one knows where the truth may be;
when I think I had a gun
and never killed anybody
and I went through hungrily enough
and I went three bloody awful long days
condemned to death
and had the whole world before me
and swapped it for a little hole in my native ground;

then I say:
'Ah God, how great Thou art!'

Winter

Rain, rain, in the poor man's house,
likewise in my heart rain.

Pain in the calloused hand,
pain of people frozen
to death on the roads.
Pain of the old and young.
Pain of the disinherited,
the deprived.

Affliction of the wounded outsider.
Pain of the prisoners,
those who suffer injustice
and live under avarice.

Affliction and struggle
for each lament I hear.
In my heart, oppressed,
sad, deep and silent,
a river of love is moving.

Rain, rain, in the poor man's house,
likewise in my heart rain.

Roots

The roots are pushing me forward.
The distant ancestors of the oak woods,
the mysterious mothers meditating
in the sunlight of precursory dawns.

When my voice was just a silence
in the caressing evening, their names
were already pulsing, running in the air.
You may not believe it, but I remember
how the lineage of my blood was born
in the woods of a long distant night
pregnant with doves and rivers.
And I too am a root, the father
of things sleeping under time,
waiting some day to flower
beneath the impassive map of this heaven.

No

If I'd said yes,
everything's OK,
the world's quite OK,
everything's hunky-dory…
Conformity.
Admiration.
Quiet, quiet, quiet
and a lot of precaution.
If I'd said perhaps
things are as they are
because they *are*,
there it is,
no point arguing.
(If he's up
and he's down,
that's life
and if some go from door to door
with a sack of ash on their shoulders,
it's because they're thick.)
If I'd said yes…
That would have been the moment
for serious conversation about
battles of flowers
in the church festivals.

But no.

Orphan with Horses behind Him

The horses of night passed over
and dawn came.
Mother,
this is the land of tears.
The horses of night passed over,
galloping.
Mother,
this is the land of grief.
Like a single glow-worm
I'd like to be,
full of light on the footpaths.
The horses of night passed over
like a black wind.
Mother,
the horses made me an orphan.

Other Names Were Given to Me

Longoreléi, chesmanéi,
when I think you are a dream,
I weep for you, for the child
you were one day,
dead of cold at the door
of a star.
Longoreléi.
There was a rumour of ice
on the faces of men.
The sun was as sad
as an anthill
and the wandering wind
was passing like a train
through the heart of midnight.
Come, love of the world,
we shall lift up the tears
of those who are cast down.
The vengeance of centuries
is at hand. The sordid
will die. Dawns
of flags and woodlands
will come like swallows.
Longoreléi, chesmanéi.

Fallen by the Sea

The proletarian language of my people,
I speak it because I do, because I like to,
it appeals to me, I love it, I want it,
because it wells up in me from the depths
of a bitter sadness which takes me over
at the sight of so many hard-hearted imbeciles,
little rootless Johnny-come-nobodies
who, when they push out their scribblings,
don't know how to base themselves
on the love of their predecessors,
how to speak the mother tongue,
the tongue of our dead grandfathers,
and to be, head high,
sailors and labourers in the language,
oar and plough, prow and ploughshare for ever.

I speak it because I do, because I like it
and want to be with my own, with my people,
close to the good men who have suffered long enough
a history told in another tongue.

I don't speak for the powerful,
I don't speak for the mean and mighty,
I don't speak for the swells,
I don't speak for the empty,
I don't speak for the stupid,
but I do speak for those who firmly bear
daily lies and injustice,
for those who sweat and weep
a daily grief of reverses,

of light and wind upon their naked eyes.
I cannot keep my words away from
the suffering of this world.
And you live in this world, land of mine,
cradle of my lineage,
Galicia, sweet affliction of Spain,
fallen by the sea, this highway…

My Kingdom

I am the king of myself.
I govern my heart
in the freedom of the wind and roads.
I obey my own laws
and follow my decrees to the letter.
A sceptre of sunsets,
a crown of passing clouds,
a scarlet mantle
of hopes and dreams
in each clean daybreak,
give me the legitimate power of the people.
I represent the silent,
I interpret those who were
the voices of the motherland
in the ancestral councils of longing.
I am a king.
A farm-hand in the days of the sputnik.

The Family Grain Store

Of that lost Eden I only have
in the mist of memory a little family grain store.
A world, an enormous world,
in the loved, warm evenings of autumn.

There was the fireside, there was the office,
there were the theatre and comics.

There, navigations and voyages,
there, ballads and stories.

I played at being a man, unaware
that my play was really very sad.

It all passed. Life
went through time, turning somersaults.

I have forgotten everything. I only remember
that Eden in the shadow of the grain store.

Poetry Is Truth

One tracks down truth
on every road, under stones,
in the obscure origins of looks,
beyond the sea spray and twilight.

I look for the truth within you, vigorous poetry
of men who labour,
real touch of things
which exist and are, though nobody sees them.
Total man,
who come and go with no shadow
along the streets
and have your truth on the heights
of the world, in the depths of history,
in the experience of some day or other,
and can't see the birds or clouds,
nor the distant hands of the harmless wind
which have caressed the world for ever.
Investigate the truth of your own time
and you will find your poetry.

Incomplete Ballad

Fuco Pérez, bastard born,
lived in Gargamala,
widower getting on a bit,
owner of a she-goat,
a bit of land that gave him
one or two potatoes.
Fuco Pérez, bastard born,
furibund iconoclast,
father of a crippled kid
stood outside his shanty.
As a stubborn nonconformist,
cops have got you spotted;
unbelieving heretic,
you are marked by pious ladies.
Fuco Pérez, bastard born,
no one knows what's up with you.
You've got the night,
you've got the morn,
you've got the little birds at dawn,
you've got the heaven's skyways,
you've got the little village streets,
you've also got the highways.
Fuco Pérez, bastard born,
what haven't you got?

Memory

Perhaps you were only a memory,
born as a memory from the opening
of a far-off night
of rain, wind and blood.

Dogs were barking from I don't know where.
But where was God in those moments
in which I was as fixed as a mountain
with a telegram throbbing in my purse
(stop) of ultimate secrets?

You were only a memory, I say, the smoke
of a fire lit in the back of beyond
of the world, over the snow,
under a noise of fishes and ants.

I'm still here and you, memory,
are not. You vanished across the river
like a fugitive dove flying
over rye-fields of wind,
giving yourself and vanishing,
the circular rattle of the sea on the delicate beach.

Time Surprised

Some morning or other
I saw the rain of time hanging
sadly from the wind
like a clothes-line of inconsolable grief
covering the ancient solitude of men.

And I saw myself for what I was:
a motionless thing, a stone of love,
with a name for others, but with no name
of my own, lacking a word
to call or define myself,
frozen out from the masks all around,
which bit by bit are grabbing at me,
making me into a stranger.

I can't find myself. In the world
I am fixed on the hill-tops,
helplessly beaten down on the roads.
I respect, I obey, I comply with the law of gravity
which weighs me down with implacable swords,
but I only know I keep on dying
a life of dreams, asking for
the why of the fire and stars,
the why of the sea on warm evenings.

A shackled shadow, I come and go,
I caper, I go forward, I fool about endlessly,
strapped to death along the long rivers
carrying the rumours of ages
like the spindrift of moans on the sierra.

I would like to redeem myself for my land,
shatter the slavery which destroys me
and be a free man, steered
by folk-songs lit like beacons.
To the north-west of the distant dun plains,
by the sea, is my land.
Eternally green,
carpeted by flowers and smiles,
woven with songs and gentle waters,
bagpipes rock its cradle of centuries
in the dense oak woods
full of voices, in the pine trees
with their deep bass notes in the motionless air,
in the villages lost in the mist;
and a noise of flutes and tambourines
lays the gold of sunset on the hills,
lifting the upward flight of the skylarks.
But beneath so much beauty
runs a deep vein of sadness,
weeping light with tears of estrangement.
Here also time carries on
digging its secret tunnel,
through which passes death, deaf,
like a black mole of nowhere.

An irresistible force which pushes me
from distant wells,
time surprised gave me the key
to the mysterious language spoken by God
and shoved dark ants into my hands.
Some morning or other.

A Poor Man on a City Street

He stretched his hand out to give me
alms of rain and cold wind.
He wasn't begging, he was giving.
His eyes slowly went over
my decent clothes.
Cars raced past,
spitting their snarls like blind beasts.

Loudspeakers, floodlit adverts
along night's dark roads,
like birds, alive for one moment
and in another dead on the frost.
He stretched his hand out timidly,
a scarcely human hand,
shyly open, like a wing
that wants to fly and can't.
He wasn't begging, he was giving.
He was giving his reasons, the oldest of the lot:
the injustice of hunger. Sadness,
the absolute solitude of the rocks.

It's your air and mine, he said
without saying it, talking with pupils
which again slowly descended on
my decent clothing.

I felt embarrassed by my clean hands
and straightaway was born in my shoes
a contrition for my waterproof soles
which stole up my veins, kept climbing
— ivy at dawn, tree at night —
to hide in my dreams for ever.

Brothers

Many men walk by my side.
I do not know them. Strangers to me.
But you, who are found far away,
over the deserts, over the lakes,
over savannahs, over islands,
I speak to as a brother.
If your night is my night,
if my eyes cry your tears,
if our griefs are the same,
I speak as a brother.
Though our words may be different,
you black and I white,
if we bear the same wounds,
I speak as a brother.
Beyond all the frontiers,
beyond walls and embankments,
if our dreams are the same,
I speak as a brother.
The same is our homeland,
the same is our struggle.
I give you my hand,
I speak as a brother.

I Can Never Forget

The sad news came through the air
and this happened: I was a pure dream,
but morning came to wake me up
and reduce me to a number adding up
to two steel boot-heels on my shoes,
which trampled across the grief of the humble.
Then I learned what blood was,
what cruelty, what zoology.
I learned metaphysics in the mountains,
physics from the fear in the valleys.
I had cold iron before my eyes
under a grim mist of worms.
This happened and I almost don't remember,
but can never forget.
I only know this, that the drums
rolled rat-a-tat, rat-a-TAT,
and I was never a dream again.

Hunger

They were two old women and a child.
They plodded up every day,
picking their way bit by bit
through the rubble of the smashed houses.
While we were eating on a corner
of the street, they used to wait,
in silence, concentrated, apart,
like withered flowers. The boy
talked to the soldiers.
The mess orderlies dragged
the black greasy cauldrons
to the doorway and threw all
the leftovers in them.
The old women and the boy
filled up their tins and went
as they had come, plodding off
bit by bit, like three black things
vanishing into the strange landscape,
swallowed by the black mouth of the air-raid shelter.

The Oppressed

Night brushed
our shoulder-length hair of tears.
The sweat of blood bubbled
like a river through our veins.
If anyone could hear our heart,
he would hear a sea in turmoil,
he would hear children crying,
mothers mourning,
crowds of voices gathered on a dark and boundless frontier.
Night rained on the pupils
of those who had frozen to death.
Those hands, moulded to stroke doves,
to grip axles and hammers,
to play harps and winds,
were broken.
Despairs came like crows
and flew far away
and then our hearts were full.

Index of Titles/First Lines

86	A Poor Man on a City Street
8	A Time to Weep
55	Baptism of Blood
87	Brothers
37	*Cantiga de Amigo* for Joan Miró
64	Christmas Eve in Harlem
18	Credo
57	Don't Look at Me
34	Eulogy for the Stonemasons
42	Exile
77	Fallen by the Sea
41	Formentor
62	Fragment of a Letter to a Poet Living in Madrid
20	Freely
65	Goethe
28	Hope
89	Hunger
88	I Can Never Forget
69	I'm a Halfwit
82	Incomplete Ballad
51	It Will Be Here
60	I Want to Go to Lugo
21	Lament for Carles Riba
33	Letter to My Wife
7	Long Night of Stone
50	María Soliña
83	Memory
29	Monologue of an Old Workman
66	Municipal Cemetery
79	My Kingdom
74	No
71	Now Is the Time to Think
30	Once
75	Orphan with Horses behind Him
76	Other Names Were Given to Me
53	Pessimistic Romance at the End of the Year
81	Poetry Is Truth

67	Prometheus Bound
27	Pure Air
26	Rabid Dog
73	Roots
10	Soldier
16	Spiritual
25	Testimony
14	The Building
44	The Fable of the Man and the Wolf
80	The Family Grain Store
39	The Heart of the Wind
47	The Honourable Men
59	The Journey Back
9	The Kingdom
90	The Oppressed
32	The Shadow
52	The Silence of God
49	The Stone
56	The Tree
84	Time Surprised
23	While We Are Walking
72	Winter
31	Words of Advice
58	You and Me

Jack Hill
was born in 1941 in the Leicestershire village of Burbage and educated at Hinckley Grammar School and St John's College, Oxford. He subsequently taught at universities in England and abroad. He first visited Galicia as a pilgrim in 1982 and later lived for periods in Noia, Santiago and Coruña. He has published several critical anthologies of his translations from different languages, including Galician, as well as volumes of his own poetry. He is the translator of two anthologies of Galician poetry, *Contemporánea* (which can be downloaded for free) and *To Visit Me the Sea* (which he edited). He lives in Essex.

GALICIAN
CLASSICS

1. Lois Pereiro,
   Collected Poems

2. Álvaro Cunqueiro,
   Folks From Here and There

3. Celso Emilio Ferreiro,
   Long Night of Stone

4. Rosalía de Castro,
   Galician Songs

5. Xosé María Díaz Castro,
   Halos

6. Rosalía de Castro,
   New Leaves

7. Carlos Casares,
   His Excellency

www.ingramcontent.com/pod-product-compliance
Lightning Source LLC
Chambersburg PA
CBHW032132090426
42743CB00007B/571